NDIVIDUAL POWER

dited by Heather C. Hudak

Weigl

ALGARY
w.weigl.com

Published by Weigl Educational Publishers Limited
6325 10 Street SE
Calgary, Alberta, Canada
T2H 2Z9

Website: www.weigl.com
Copyright ©2009 Weigl Educational Publishers Limited

All of the Internet URLs given in the book were valid at the time of publication. However, due to the
dynamic nature of the Internet, some addresses may have changed, or sites may have ceased to exist
since publication. While the author and publisher regret any inconvenience this may cause readers,
no responsibility for any such changes can be accepted by either the author or the publisher.

Library and Archives Canada Cataloguing in Publication data available upon request.
Fax (403) 233-7769 for the attention of the Publishing Records department.

ISBN 978-1-55388-470-5 (hard cover)
ISBN 978-1-55388-471-2 (soft cover)

Printed in the United States of America
1 2 3 4 5 6 7 8 9 0 12 11 10 09 08

Photograph Credits
Every reasonable effort has been made to trace ownership and to obtain
permission to reprint copyright material. The publishers would be pleased
to have any errors or omissions brought to their attention so that they may
be corrected in subsequent printings.

Weigl acknowledges Getty Images as its primary image supplier for this title.
British Columbia Archives: page 20 top (e_05182); courtesy of Helen Siemens: page 21, 29 bottom left.

Project Coordinators: Heather C. Hudak, Heather Kissock
Design: Terry Paulhus

We acknowledge the financial support of the Government of Canada through the Book Publishing
Industry Development Program (BPIDP) for our publishing activities.

Contents

Citizenship and Individual Power

While the theory of democracy states that all people should be treated equally, experience tells us that in practice this is not always the case. Canadians can use the media and interest groups to affect political decision making, but do all people have an equal chance to do so? In most cases, the answer is no.

When people are denied access to those who make policy decisions and enact the laws by which they must live, they are quite powerless. Yet access alone is not enough. The ability to exert political pressure determines whose concerns and interests will be reflected in public debate and government policy. In order to take full advantage of the chance to influence decision makers, citizens must have both resources and skills.

Several factors enhance or diminish a citizen's chances of acquiring those skills, resources, and access to power in Canada. An individual's empowerment is affected by socio-economic factors, cultural factors, geographical factors, and **demographic** factors. Understanding how these can work for or against us is an important step in learning to exercise our full rights as Canadian citizens.

Tuktoyaktuk is a small community north of the Arctic Circle along the coast of the Arctic Ocean.

ographical factors can enhance or
rict an individual's power. Not only
lifestyles and opinions vary from place
place, but citizenship does as well. A
son living in Tuktoyaktuk, Northwest
ritories, may have different interests
d views than someone growing up in
onto, Ontario. Though both are
nadians, each views citizenship in a
erent way. Each faces unique challenges
en it comes to obtaining the skills and
ources needed to interact with those in
itions of power.

nada's large landmass holds a relatively
all population. The country's immense
d area and dispersed population affect
v Canadians exercise their citizenship.
turally, physical distance can bring
h it psychological distance. While
nadian citizens living in Ottawa can
ily gather together on Parliament
 if they want to protest a federal
rernment decision, people in the Yukon
ght feel remote, forgotten, and too far
y to be heard. People in the Yukon
ght also feel they lack the numbers
nfluence federal decisions.

hough Canada boasts a vast
graphical area, the majority of
nadians live in the southern quarter
he country, and about 60 percent
ll Canadians live in Ontario and
ebec. Individual power and influence
government is affected by the physical
ance between those who govern and
se who are governed.

graphic diversity also challenges
sense of national unity that can
ngthen a country. Canadians who live
usands of miles apart in landscapes
l communities profoundly unlike each
er may feel they have little in common.

More than 7.5 million people live in the province of Quebec.

Think About It

Sometimes, citizens are affected by situations that seem outside
their reach. How can these citizens increase their power to gain
control over events that affect them? What steps could political
leaders take to make themselves more accessible?

Canada's Geographical Regions

Canada's population, posted at more than 33 million at last census, is spread across nearly 1 million square kilometres of varying land forms, climates, and resources. This large area can be divided into six regions based on land forms, resources and industry, and political boundaries.

The Atlantic Provinces include New Brunswick, Nova Scotia, Prince Edward Island, and Newfoundland and Labrador.

In this region, most of the population liv where agriculture and fishing are the ma industries. In the low mountains inland, forestry and mining have been develope

The Great Lakes-St. Lawrence Lowlands region extends across the southern tips of Ontario and Quebec. It is sometimes called the "heartland" of Canada becaus people, industry, and agriculture aboun More than half of Canada's population lives in this region, and nearly 75 percen

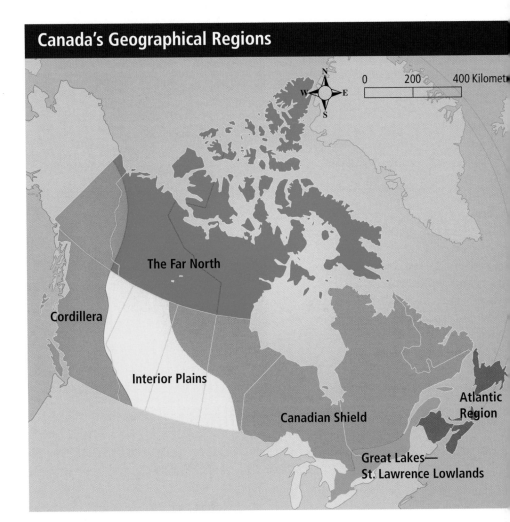

Canada's Geographical Regions

The Far North

Cordillera

Interior Plains

Canadian Shield

Atlantic Region

Great Lakes—
St. Lawrence Lowlands

0   200   400 Kilomet

the total value of the country's
manufactured goods are produced here.
well, the area's good quality soil and
ld climate support intensive agriculture.

e Canadian Shield is a geographical
gion that spans nearly half of Canada's
inland. It includes the northern parts
Quebec, Ontario, Manitoba, and
skatchewan. Its landscape ranges
om bare ancient rocks to dense forests
d lakes. The small population lives in
mmunities that rely on the Shield's
tural resources, such as minerals, wood,
d water power, for their industry.

e Interior Plains is the largest stretch
nearly level land in Canada. Large grain
ms and ranches are plentiful here, and
e size and location of cities depends on
e number of farmers in an area who
ed urban goods and services. Wheat
d petroleum are the best-known
oducts in this region.

e Cordillera includes British Columbia
d the Yukon. Three-quarters of its
pulation and its major cities are in
uthwestern British Columbia. Most of
e area is mountainous, so agriculture is
ited to narrow valleys and flood plains.

The region is important for natural
resources, such as forest products,
minerals, and fish.

The Far North is a diverse area defined
more by political boundaries than by
geography or economics. The population
is small, and few of its resources, mainly
minerals, have been developed because of
the climate and huge distances. Some
people rely on hunting, fishing, and
trapping for all or part of their livelihood.

The Quebec-Windsor Axis

The most populous region in Canada is a narrow strip of cities
known to demographers as the Quebec-Windsor axis. Roughly
1,100 kilometres long and varying between 160 and 240
kilometres deep, this corridor occupies less than 2 percent of
Canada's landmass. It is home, however, to nearly 60 percent
of all Canadians. The 10 urban metropolitan centres in the axis,
including the nation's capital, account for more than half the
national population. Therefore, its economic and social interests
are obviously of great importance to those in power. With
representation by population, there is little concern about
being forgotten in the House of Commons.

WEB LINK

Visit **www.canadiangeographic.com/atlas/
intro.aspx?lang=En to learn more about Canada's geography.**

Urban-Rural Split

Different geographical regions tend to have different problems. The economic activity supporting a region is usually tied to the landscape, as are the number and type of people living there.

Although Canada is a huge country, nearly 90 percent of its landmass is without permanent settlement. Today, most Canadians live in cities. A century ago, three out of four lived in rural communities or on farms.

Life in urban Canada brings with it a different type of citizenship than life in rural Canada. It is often much easier to draw a group of city people together because the distance to travel is not so

great as in the country. It might also be less expensive for people in urban areas to hold meetings, protests, or public events. City dwellers may spend less on transportation to attend public meeting and might also save money on phone ca and emails needed to organize and inqu about meetings.

There is the danger that politicians will pay more attention to the regions of the country that are most populated. By catering to the majority of people in the regions, politicians hope to be elected.

Interests in urban and rural Canada can be quite different. If politicians favour o region over another, a whole section of

ple could be overlooked because
their geographical location. If that
pens, those people must struggle even
re to influence government decisions.

term "urbanization" refers to the
wth of a country's communities.
en the cities or towns in a country
ome larger, more specialized, and
re interdependent, the process
urbanization is underway. With
anization comes changes in **society**,
ether they are economic, technological,
itical, or demographic. In Canada,
anization varies from one region
nother because of geographic and
nomic factors. Quebec, Ontario, and
ish Columbia are the most urbanized
vinces. They have the population and
nomic resources needed to build larger
es and towns. However, Canada's
an population has not always been so
centrated. The growth of cities and
ns has occurred in several stages over
ny years.

first stage began about the time
ebec was founded in 1608. Great
tain and France controlled Canada's
led lands at that time. These two
ntries directed the location, function,
l growth of cities such as Halifax, St.
n's, Quebec City, and Montreal. Most
e military bases or administration
tres. They were places where goods
ld be distributed, but they lacked
to other towns in the area and
ended mainly on water transportation.
en these cities first developed, they
ained under the control of Great
tain and France.

second stage of development occurred
en trade and commerce in Canada
anded in the early 1800s. In Canada,
ional markets took on a new

importance. Citizens began producing
some goods to sell locally, and cities
became centres of regional commerce.
New transportation methods, such as
steamships and railways, appeared, and
cities began to look more organized, with
separate residential and commercial areas.

The third stage began in the 1870s,
during the Industrial Revolution, and
ended in the 1920s. During this time,
power became concentrated in a number
of large cities, including Toronto and
Montreal. Technological changes altered
the look of urban areas and created new
jobs. Tall office towers loomed over cities
that spread out into suburbs. Huge
factories emerged.

The fourth phase occurred from the
1940s to the 1970s. The automobile
became better and more popular, and
the focus changed from products to
services. Corporate growth was tied to
major cities and Canada's population
increased. Shopping centres, downtown
office towers, high-rise apartments and
industrial parks became main features
of Canadian cities.

The urbanization of Canada, which
consistently drew rural people, slowed
after the 1970s. An energy crisis and
high interest rates were responsible.
In city centres, the population remained
static or declined. In areas around cities,
population grew. Cities began losing
people to the country.

What Can You Do?

Rural population is declining. How do you think this factor affects
government policies for rural areas? How might people in rural
areas try to influence government decisions?

Active Citizenship: Dividing the Northwest Territories

Geography and **culture** can have a powerful impact on the amount of influence people have on government decisions. In an effort to gain more control over decisions that affect them, Inuit people in northern Canada sought more control over their own government. They wanted the Northwest Territories to be divided, creating two new political regions.

For many years, Inuit people living in the eastern Arctic dreamed of governing themselves in their own language. They wanted to make laws and decisions that were sensitive to their unique region,

With the formation of Nunavut, Inuit people have been able to better preserve their cultural heritage.

ere people rode dog sleds one day
d sat at computers the next. They
nted to decide how to manage
ir own wildlife, and how to educate
ir children.

May 4, 1992, about 26,000 people
oss the Northwest Territories went
he polling booths to vote on whether
y wanted their territory divided in two.
iding the territory would create two
w territories. One would keep the name
rthwest Territories, and the second
uld be called *Nunavut*, a word meaning
ur land" in the Inuktitut language.
navut would include 2 million square
ometres of land in the eastern Arctic,
h about 350,000 square kilometres
that owned by the Inuit in the region.
navut's population would include
ut 20,000 Inuit people, and the new
ritory would have its own legislature.
it people would account for the
jority of the people in the region,
the Inuit would be able to make many
the political decisions that affect them.

en voters arrived at the polls, they were
en a 186-word question written in eight
guages. A map was also provided to
w where the division would be made.
wever, the results of the vote, called
lebiscite, did not have to be put into
ce by politicians in Ottawa and the
rthwest Territories. The vote was a
asure of public opinion on the issue.

hink About It

entify the roles that geography
nd culture played in the Northwest
rritories' boundary dispute. How did the
eation of Nunavut and a new, Inuit-led
overnment improve life for people in the
astern Arctic?

Voter turnout was high across the region,
and 54 percent voted in favour of creating
Nunavut. A great deal of controversy
surrounded the vote, however. Three out
of every four Inuit people in the Arctic
were illiterate, and these people needed
help reading the question on the ballot.
As well, many people thought the lengthy
question was not clear or suitable. In
addition, voters from the western Arctic
were voting on the future of a region they
might never have visited.

On top of all this, the vote seemed to
pit one half of the Arctic's people against
the other half. Most of the people in the
eastern Arctic were Inuit and in favour
of division, while many non-Aboriginal
Peoples, Metis, and Dene lived in the
western Arctic and were against division.
Many people in the western Arctic argued
that the creation of Nunavut would be
costly and unnecessary. They were
concerned that having two governments
to represent only 55,000 people would not
be efficient. As well, the Dene opposed the
division because the boundary would cut
across their hunting and burial grounds.

By mid-1992, politicians in the Northwest
Territories and Ottawa were both firmly
behind the creation of Nunavut. The Inuit
wanted control over their homeland, and
the federal government wanted to prove
its concern for Aboriginal issues. In fact,
the federal Indian Affairs Department said
the division would happen regardless of
the public vote.

In 1993, the federal government passed
the Nunavut Act, which became official
six years later. Today, about 30,000 people
live in the territory. It has 28 communities,
three national parks, and the capital city
is Iqaluit.

Socio-economic Factors in Power

Socio-economic factors play an important role in determining Canadians' power to affect decision making. Socio-economic factors include income, gender, occupation, and education. All of these affect the social or economic standing of the citizen. How much money citizens make, the type of jobs they hold, and the amount of education they have all affect their ability to influence people in power or gain positions of power in society.

As a social group, those who are less fortunate are often unable to participate fully in the life of the community, and as a result, they are less able to influence decision making.

Poverty is a complex issue with many causes. People are unable to be self-supporting for a number of reasons. Personal misfortunes, such as illness, accidents, family breakdown, or death can limit people's ability to support themselves, as can a lack of education or job skills, cultural or language barriers, or age.

One survey by Statistics Canada showed that a typical Canadian family used 43 percent of its income to pay personal taxes, transportation, and shelter costs. More than 12 percent of families and about 40 percent of unattached individuals were considered to have low incomes.

ple who spend all their time struggling
meet basic needs are less likely to take
t in political decision making. It is
ier for people to work at political
vities when they have the time and
ney to devote to them. What this
ans is that more than three million
nadians are less likely to participate
political decision making due to their
nomic status.

other socio-economic factor is the
erent income levels across Canada.
example, Canadians in the Atlantic
vinces have, on average, have incomes
t are lower than in other parts of
nada. These differences in income
ween the regions of Canada exist for
umber of reasons, but the main factors
the differences in employment levels
l wage rates.

tistics Canada keeps track of the
nbers of workers in each region, the
nber of those employed, and the wages
d for various jobs. The result is that
y are able to compare regions based on
proportion of employed workers.

antic Canada has had a lower
rage income than other regions
to a smaller proportion of workers
he total population and the large
centage of unemployed. This accounts
some of the gap in average income
ween regions.

People in some parts of Canada have more money to spend.

In 2006, Statistics Canada reported that
the average Canadian family had an
income of $58,300. Newfoundland and
Labrador had the lowest average family
income at $45,800, while Alberta had the
highest at $70,500. While there are no
complete answers as to how these statistics
are related to political power in Canada,
it is clear that they are related. The main
struggle among the different provinces
and the federal government over the past
60 years has been to balance economic
and political power among the provinces.
Citizens in some regions of the country
perceive that they have less power than
those in others, and this has had a negative
affect on their ability to participate fully in
the decision-making process.

What Can You Do?

though Canada is a relatively
ealthy country, many people live
poverty. How much power does a
omeless person have in Canadian

society? How could such a person
have an influence on political
decision making?

Talk about recent news coverage of
political and issues. What issues

can you identify as regional
concerns? Atlantic Canada relies on
the fishing industry for much of its
employment. What would happen
to the Atlantic economy if fish
stocks continued to decline?

ducation and Literacy

ne of the factors that affects the way
a citizen participates in society is
person's level of education. Early
rmers in Canada thought a publicly-
led education system would be one
to defeat poverty and crime. The
ry was that people who had been
ated would not choose to live such a
Mostly, however, it was thought that
ation would provide citizens with
l opportunities to take part in society,
rdless of their social background. In
nited way, this was true.

le all Canadian children have the
ortunity to attend school, it is not
that this gives all students an equal
ortunity. Children who grow up in
lies with below-average incomes
ht not receive regular, well-balanced
ls. Although these children are able to
nd school, their hunger may impair
r concentration, alertness, and ability
sorb information. Attending school
ly part of what is needed to get a
d education.

zens who attain high political
e almost always have a university
ation. In fact, many people claim
a university education is needed to
e decisions about the many complex
es faced by society. A look at the
kgrounds of federal MPs shows that
t have post-secondary training of
e sort. It is clear, however, that not all
ens aspire to political office. What
l of education do people need to the
c role of a citizen in politics?

politicians have a university
llege degree.

One term that people use to describe
the minimum level of education is
"functional literacy." Functional literacy
is the ability to read and write at a very
basic level, enough to be able to read bus
schedules, campaign posters, ballots,
television schedules, and the directions
for a simple machine, such as a DVD
player. About 15 percent of Canadians
are thought to be functionally illiterate.
These people may not be able to do many
jobs, and their ability to function
as citizens may be severely hindered.
Literacy is also related to other socio-
economic factors, such as poverty.
Generally speaking, it is often difficult
for people living at or below the
poverty line to take advantage
of their educational opportunities.

Power and Culture in Canada

In Canada, people's culture has affected their level of political power for hundreds of years. Canada's Aboriginal Peoples lost much of their political power in the years following European settlement. Between the earliest European trading voyages and the beginning of the nineteenth century Canada's Aboriginal Peoples lost much of their land, all their decision-making power, their political and social structures, and many of their cultural and social traditions. The Aboriginal Peoples' loss of individual power in Canada was complete, and only in the past 40 years have they been able to begin reclaiming their decision-making power in Canada.

During the early history of European settlement, British and French people struggled for power in North America. The Province of Canada was created by an act of British Parliament passed in 184⬛ The act took effect in February 1841, a⬛ joined Ontario, known as Upper Cana⬛ and Quebec, known as Lower Canada, with one government structure. The ac⬛ gave Upper and Lower Canada the sam⬛ number of seats in government. The ef⬛ of this was that French Canadian inter⬛ were underrepresented in the governm⬛ At the time of the union, there were ab⬛ 670,000 people in Lower Canada, of whom, about 510,000 were French-speaking. There were only about 480,0⬛ people in Upper Canada. The intentior⬛ the act was to submerge French-speaki⬛ interests in the new government, and g⬛ English-speaking people most of the se⬛ in any government. For the French Canadian people of the 1840s, culture played a major role in their ability to participate in political decision makin⬛

sely related to the issue of culture and
ividual power are problems associated
h language. There are many Canadians
o do not speak either English or French
a first language, and they can face many
riers to full participation in politics.
original Canadians in remote areas
Canada often speak their own
original languages, and have very
e communication with those who
not speak these languages. There are
o many Canadians of different cultural
kgrounds, and recent **immigrants** who
not speak one of the official languages.
these people have trouble participating
y in society. Anything printed by the
eral government is in either French
English. Workers in government
ces generally speak only French or
glish. Schools, colleges, and libraries
n use only English or French. In these
es, language becomes a barrier to
ticipation rather than a means of
mmunication. Citizens who neither
ak nor understand English or French
l it harder to follow political events
he media or even read brochures
m candidates. This makes it difficult
these people to be involved in politics.
wever, there are many cultural
anizations that provide translation
vices to help Canadians who do not
ak either official language. Even so, the
of another language remains a barrier
ull participation.

h year, Canadians organize cultural
ivals to promote and celebrate
ir ethnic backgrounds. Many people
ieve these festivals help citizens
lerstand and appreciate Canada's
lticultural nature, and also help
nadians feel included in society.

lay, there are hundreds of major
ivals in Canada every year.

Festivals are also used to preserve,
promote, and celebrate particular cultures
in Canada. Canada's Aboriginal Peoples
hold many festivals throughout the
country each year. Across the country,
there are now annual festivals that
celebrate Canada's diversity. Each invites
Canadians of all ethnic backgrounds to
enjoy the food and culture of different
ethnic groups.

Multicultural festivals help Canadians
of different cultures preserve their
heritage. They are a celebration of
Canadians' unique backgrounds. They
can also foster mutual respect among
Canadians, regardless of race, heritage, or
ethnic background. Many people believe
that multicultural festivals not only help
citizens feel more in touch with their
roots, but also help people accept and
appreciate Canada's diversity. Many
believe that such events provide an
opportunity for people of different
cultures to meet, and in doing so foster
a sense of unity. When people feel
accepted and included in society, they
often feel they have more power to make
their views heard.

WEB LINK
Visit www.culture.ca/featuredarticle-articlepublie-
e/cultural_festivals-festivals_culturels_200707.html
to learn more about Canada's festivals.

Gender: Women and Active Citizenship

Like ethnic minorities, it is often difficult for Canadian women to attain powerful political positions. This gender imbalance remains, even in recent years. At the outset of the 2000s, women in politics were still largely subordinate to men. In 2008, women held only about 20 percent of the seats in the House of Commons.

Although the media have given the women's movement much coverage over the years, gender inequality has remained a part of corporate Canada. For example, many of the top-ranked civil servants in Canada's crown corporations were men. Since crown corporations help design and implement many government policies and programs, the number of men in management positions gives them much more political influence than women.

Judging from a number of studies, it might seem surprising that few women hold top jobs in public office. Research shown that urban women are very activ in politics. Since most members of Parliament began their careers in lower party ranks, the statistics suggest that women will have greater access to top political jobs in the future. However, numbers often do not reveal the whole picture. A closer look at female party workers shows that women have most often been given "housekeeping and menial tasks" by their organizations.

For years, women have run **constituenc** offices, answered telephones, and processed mailouts. Men who join a ma political party, on the other hand, have had a much better chance of advancing to the highest levels. Traditionally, men

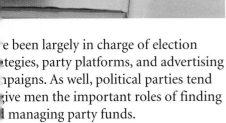

e been largely in charge of election
tegies, party platforms, and advertising
npaigns. As well, political parties tend
give men the important roles of finding
l managing party funds.

order for people to advance to public
ce, they must first gain top-level jobs
hin their political parties. Due to male
l female political roles established over
ny years, it could be many years before
der equality becomes a part of
nadian politics.

e number of women pursuing careers
oublic office has increased in recent
rs, but still relatively few are being
:ted. Political parties seem to treat male
l female members differently.

ne women, however, have by-passed
ir problems and won important
itical positions. Jeanne Sauvé's term as
aker of the House of Commons and
r as Governor General set a precedent.
r position as Speaker allowed her to
y a role in the inner workings of the

House of Commons. Since then, Adrienne
Clarkson and Michaëlle Jean have also
served as governor general.

Once women like Sauvé earn seats in the
House of Commons, they become quite
visible among the male majority. Perhaps
this is why women in the House have
tended to be quickly awarded Cabinet
posts. Still, these posts have rarely been in
the "power portfolios" of finance, industry,
trade, the treasury, or justice.

Apart from pursuing political careers,
there are many ways that women and men
can express their views and become
actively involved in society. Individual
skills and resources can be used to exert
political influence in different ways.

What Can You Do?

Think about people who have recently made a contribution
to women's equality. What did they do, and how did it help
women advance?

CITIZEN PROFILE

The Famous Five

In 1919, the Federated Women's Institut of Canada asked Prime Minister Rober Borden to appoint a woman to the Senat Two years later, the Montreal Women's Club asked Prime Minister Arthur Meighen to appoint Murphy to the Sena Meighen replied that his hands were tied—a woman was not a person, so she could not be a senator. He promised to d something about the problem and so did the next prime minister, Mackenzie King After eight years, three prime ministers, and no effective action, Murphy took matters into her own hands.

Judge Emily Murphy decided to request Supreme Court interpretation of the ter of the BNA Act. To do so, Murphy neede a petition with five signatures. The grou of women who contributed came to be known as "the famous five." In addition to Murphy, the other four members of t group were Nellie McClung, Irene Parlby Louise McKinney, and Henrietta Edward

Nellie McClung was a writer, an Alberta MLA, and a well-known champion of women's rights. She is best remembered for her fiery speeches in favour of giving women the vote. After the vote was won McClung continued her campaign to improve the lives of women and childre through such measures as fairer propert rights, public health programs, and mothers' allowances.

Irene Parlby shared many of McClung's ideas. As a cabinet minister, she support laws that helped women and children, especially in rural areas. These laws included improvements to rural schools and the assignment of more nurses to

One day in 1914, Nellie McClung led several hundred women to the Manitoba legislature to protest women's rights. Nellie made a speech. The premier listened, but he would not change his mind. Two days later, the women returned to the legislature. They acted out a play. In the play, the women pretended to be politicians and debated if they should let men vote. Nellie acted as the premier. The crowd thought the play was funny.

People's attitudes were changing. A new government was elected in 1915. The following year, Manitoba became the first Canadian province to allow women to vote.

for pregnant women in
countryside.

ise McKinney was the first woman
elected to a legislature in Canada and
he British Empire. One of her many
omplishments was to arouse public
inion against the unjust status
tment of widows and separated
es in Canadian society.

78 years old, Henrietta Edwards was
eldest member of the group. She was
urnalist who organized the Montreal
rking Girls' Association, a forerunner
he YWCA. Edwards was considered an
ert on the legal status of women. She
d the office of Convener of Laws for the
ional Council of Women.

en the Famous Five's petition arrived
Ottawa, the Supreme Court of Canada
eld the ruling that women were not
rsons." Only after the women
ealed to the Judicial Committee
he Privy Council in England
s the ruling overturned.

On October 1, 1929, Lord Sankey, Lord
Chancellor of Great Britain, delivered
the judgement: "The British North
America Act planted in Canada a living
tree capable of growth and expansion
within its natural limits... their Lordships
have come to the conclusion that the word
"person", in Section 24, includes members
of both the male and the female sex... and
that women are eligible to be summoned
to and become members of the Senate of
Canada, and they will humbly advise His
Majesty accordingly."

The judgment was a great victory
for Canadian women. Now they could
be active in all aspects of Canadian
citizenship. Their participation would
never again be challenged on the grounds
that they were not "persons."

Of course the Persons Case, as it has come
to be known, was just one step in an
ongoing struggle for women's equality.
Each year, the Government of Canada
presents a Persons Award to someone
who has improved the status of women.

e Famous Five monument in Calgary, Alberta, honours Nellie and the other women who were involved in the Persons Case.

Think About It

Each year the Government of Canada presents a Persons Award to someone who has improved the status of women. Think about people who have recently made a contribution to women's equality. Who would you choose for this year's award?

Citizens Overcoming Barriers

Citizens do not face the same challenges in trying to make decisions in society. Some are challenged by real or perceived barriers. For example, people with physical disabilities often face real barriers, such as inaccessible buildings and lack of transportation. The attitudes of others can also be a barrier. Seniors are expected by employers and family to stop working at age 65, whether they feel ready to retire or not. Young people face a similar barrier to participation when others consider them too young to take part in decision making. For both young people and seniors there may be laws or rules preventing participation because of their age. All these citizens have one thing in common—barriers to participation as citizens. These barriers are being slowly lowered as society begins to fully understand the problems.

Senior citizens are one of the fastest growing groups in Canada. This change our population's age structure is referre to as "the greying of Canada." It is partl result of the post-war baby boom, and partly due to medical advances and mo

althy living. Policy makers are beginning
consider the possible effects on
anadian society, fearing that fewer
xpayers of working age may have to
ar a heavier burden for healthcare
rvices and pension incomes. Today's
niors do not fit the old stereotypes. Most
ople remain active in the community
ng after retirement. Many seniors
votes time to charitable, service, or
lunteer organizations, and some are
rolled in university. Others have
ported being active in political
ganizations. Canada's seniors are senior
izens in every sense of the term, making
luable contributions to society.

der Canadians are concerned about
ing independent for as long as possible.
do so they need money, satisfying
ork, mental health, physical well being,
d suitable housing. Many programs and
cilities have been developed in response
their new activism. These include
ecial housing for both couples and
gles, elder hostel programs to combine
vel with education, paid tuition at
nadian universities, and social
ograms for those who live alone.
lunteer shopping, meals-on-wheels,
memaker, and repair services provide
usehold help. Home nursing care has
luced the need to hospitalize many
iors. Keeping seniors in institutions
expensive for society. By exerting their
litical influence, seniors are winning
etter quality of life which benefits
Canadians.

ople with physical and mental
abilities also face many barriers,
ecially in the workplace. Their income
els are often low. Many men and
men with disabilities are employed as
nual workers. Unemployment is a
mmon problem, because people with

disabilities are much more likely than
other adult Canadians to be without work.
It has been said that unemployment is the
most limiting factor for many people
trying to enjoy full citizenship. It is
important for people with disabilities to
have a means of self-support, and to be
able to contribute their knowledge and
skills to society.

Think About It

Like other groups with limited finances, it is often hard for people
with disabilities to persuade those in power to make their needs
a priority. What challenges do people with disabilities face?

Children and Society

Historically, the very young have had little influence on the society in which they live. Children have been left out of most decision making because many adults think of them as uninformed and disinterested. However, improving education and new technology have allowed children to acquire skills and knowledge at an earlier age. Television has played a major role in shaping children's awareness of society.

Researchers studying the effects of these changes on children in many countries have uncovered both predictable and surprising facts about their political attitudes and activities. Even very young children have been able to assess what they see and hear on political issues. Their views are often quite distinct from those of the adults around them. In community-based studies that polled people of various ages on specific issues, the young also had different priorities. They insisted on the need for peace; on using resources to end poverty, hunger, and homelessness; and on immediate action to safeguard the environment. Children felt strongly that their countries should give more help to developing nations, even if it meant a decrease in their own standard of living.

Many Canadian schools are working to get children involved in important issues. In one western Canadian city, students built birdhouses to attract purple martins to local parks. The area had a mosquito problem, and the bug-eating birds greatly reduced the need for pesticides. A local trust company provided funds, publicity, and materials. The entire community benefited from this response to a real environmental problem.

Individual children across Canada have also been using their skills and enthusiasm to contribute to society. Many have started or worked with recycling projects, such as picking up used telephone books, cans and bottles, or newspapers.

Children are naturally lacking many of the resources and skills that adult Canadians command. However, they do have the same needs and require support, attention, and access to services and tax dollars. These citizens need to live safe lives, so that they can grow to their full potential. It is important that children be included in research, discussions, and group projects that explore new approaches to ongoing problems. The expression of childrens' unique views and priorities can benefit society as a whole.

What is Your Viewpoint?

Should minority groups in Canada be protected? Canadian citizens are supposed to have the same ability to influence and participate in political decision making. These four fictional citizens have different viewpoints about the power of minorities in Canada. Read each of the viewpoints and discuss them with your classmates.

Viewpoint #1
Immigrants have no business complaining about conditions in Canada.

I just don't get it. I thought people came to Canada because it was so much better than where they were! Nobody forced them to come to Canada. Sure, immigrants have rights like everyone else, but don't they expect a bit too much? My grandparents came here as immigrants, and they had to work for years to establish themselves. There weren't any government training programs, either. They had to teach themselves how to speak English, and they didn't expect to have the same as everyone else in their first year here. I think new immigrants should be happier with the way things are and spend less time thinking about how things could be perfect.

Viewpoint #2
My people have been here longer than anyone.

Aboriginal Peoples have waited too long for proper treatment in this country. Although the Canadian government treated some ethnic minorities poorly, many of them were able to participate in politics before we were. Until the 1960s, we had to give up our traditions and rights to be able to vote. We were the first citizens of this country, and we are among the last to be able to effectively participate in political decision making.

wpoint #3
st don't think there's a real problem. ink the media plays it up.

ivists are always stirring things up, and media comes along and broadcasts it I don't believe half of it. When you boil ght down, we're all racists in one way nother, so what's the big deal? As long mmigrants get everything they're posed to, I don't see what all the fuss bout. I think people get treated pretty l in this country, and I don't think it's essary to stir things up.

Viewpoint #4
Canadians have to try to live together in peace and justice.

I don't think private citizens or public officials should tolerate racist attitudes or policies. We live in a free and democratic country that is the envy of much of the world. We are seen to be a peace-loving nation. It is unthinkable that anyone should be barred from employment or elected office in Canada because of skin colour, race, or creed. Every Canadian should be prepared take a stand on behalf of any other. If Canadians want to achieve the goal of unity in diversity, they will have to develop a more positive attitude to minorities, and a greater understanding of their problems.

Take the Citizenship Challenge

How do multicultural festivals improve relations between people, regardless of their ethnic background. How might a multicultural festival improve a person's power to influence decisions in society?

1. Identify the types of activities that a multicultural festival might include. How might such events foster a sense of unity among people? How might they give people more power over decisions that affect them?

2. Discuss how you would organize such a festival. Who would participate? How long would the festival be? Where would it be held? How would you go about organizing the festival?

3. Imagine you are organizing a multicultural festival at your school. Discuss which events would best help empower students in your school. Wr two or three possible programs for th festival. Eliminate the programs that least effective in empowering student and choose the festival program that you feel would be best.

4. Why do you think is it important for Canadians to be aware of events and conditions in other countries? Write paragraph explaining your answer, an share it with friends.

Q What are Canada's six regions?

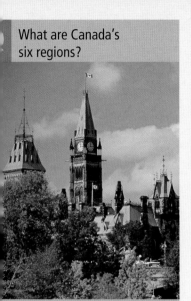

A Atlantic Provinces, Great Lakes-St. Lawrence Lowlands, Canadian Shield, Interior Plains, Cordillera, the Far North

Q What does the term "urbanization" mean?

A urbanization refers to the growth of a country's communities

Q What are socio-economic factors?

A income, gender, occupation, and education

Q Who were the Famous Five?

A Emily Murphy, Nellie McClung, Irene Parlby, Louise McKinney, and Henrietta Edwards

Q Traditionally, what jobs have women played in politics?

A housekeeping and menial tasks

Q What are three groups of Canadians that face real or perceived barriers?

A senior citizens, young people, and people with disabilities

Further Research

Suggested Reading

Drexler, Kateri M., and Gwen Garcelon. *Strategies for Active Citizenship*. Toronto: Pearson Education, 2004.

Pezzi, Bryan. *Nellie McClung*. Calgary: Weigl Education Publishers Limited, 2008.

Wells, Don (ed.). *Canadian Citizenship* (Canadian Government series). Calgary: Weigl Educational Publishers Limited, 2005.

Internet Resources

See what's being done to encourage active citizenship within Canada by visiting the Institute for Canadian Citizenship at **www.icc-icc.ca**

Find out more about Canadian women in politics at **www.cbc.ca/news/interactives/map-cda-womenpolitics**

Learn more about the Famous Five organization at **www.abheritage.ca/famous5**

lossary

stituency: the people living
ithin a political district
ho have the right to send a
presentative to government

ture: the ideas, beliefs, values,
nd knowledge that make up the
asis of social action

nographic: having to do
ith the statistical study
f human populations and
nformation, such as births,
eaths, population density,
istribution, and migration

functional literacy: the ability to
read and write at a very basic
level, enough to cope in society

immigrants: people into a country
for settlement purposes

plebiscite: a public vote that is not
binding on the government but
intended to measure public
opinion on an issue

society: a system of human
organization that generates
distinct cultural patterns
and institutions

Index